DBrockman Publishing *White*

Presents

"I Did It All In Black And White"

White

Published by DBrockman Publishing

"I did it all in Black and White"
Copyrights © Keasha Gray 2011
All rights reserved. Printed in the United States of America. No part of this may be reproduced and or transmitted in any form or by any means without written permission by the author, except in the case of brief quotations embodied in critical articles and reviews. Contact:

DBrockman Publishing,
5414 Fountain Pk Blvd
Tampa, Fl 33617
dbpublisher@yahoo.com

Important Publisher Note:
    The materials in this book represent the person of the author and not to be applicable to all situations. Many circumstances appear similar, but differ in respects
    Each reader should use caution in applying any material contained in this book to his other specific circumstance, and should seek advice of an appropriate professional.
    (Author's note: Use your common sense!)

~~BLACK~~

White

DBrockman's Dedication (Love You Keash)

If the strongest vessel in my body was taken and reduced
to the lowest terms.
I still wouln't be able to simplify the things I've gathered
from you and how my heart yearns.

A moonless night without the stars shining bright you
still would be more than my guiding light.
Without an ocean filled with tide, and no waves to take
a ride, you still surf thru my mind as wind blows a kite.

If I had to choose my battles I would be a fougthless soul
trying to figure out how all of this came about.
I remember the trip to the O hanging with the fellows,
and in your dress you stood out.

From that night the chances we took many may not
understand, but thus is why we're here today,
Within the 2nd 48 we were on an escape, still don't
memba falling asleep and part of the things that happen
in M.I.A

That was just the tip of there berg, remember that night
on the beach in the Burg, that was exciting,
I couldn't have asked for what you provide, I just know
what I feel deep inside, I'll be the bolt and you the
lightning.

Hope you enjoy these memories a lifetime, sure there
would be more times, but I will end this for now,
This book is dedicated to you Keasha Gray, the love I
have for you will stay, and I will never question How?

White

White

i did it all in black and white

gray, keasha

~~BLACK &~~ *White*

3   adventure

BLACK & White

A
db
dbrockman publishing

4   adventure

~~BLACK &~~ *White*

5   adventure

~~BLACK~~ & ~~White~~
your favorite colors

Keasha Gray *August 8, 2010 at 7:22pm*

with so many colors
that remind me of you.
i chose to use two
a brown and a blue.

the brown for our bodies
when they become intertwined.
the blue for my feelings
when your not by my side.

the brown is so sexy
my heart skips a beat.
the blue makes me feel
like my life is incomplete.

light blue or dark
it doesn't matter what shade
because brown is the color
that our bodies made.

although the blue
doesn't bring me much joy
i'll take the blue with the brown
because they are both yours.

~~BLACK~~ & ~~White~~
told i would do the mirror thing lol

Keasha Gray *August 10, 2010 at 11:35am*

i think im running out of inspiration. i wrote this but it doesnt give me the feeling that i want when i read it. hope you enjoy it anyway.

i see my thoughts
and my fears
my happiness
and my tears
i havent felt this way in years.

i see my past
and all my flaws
every time i caught a football
that run in i had with the law
cant close my eyes, i see it all.

i see my boys
ages 14 and 4
whom i truly adore
with my hearts core
each day makes my love grow more and more.

but seeing these things
that are all about me
are scary as can be
listen close and you'll see

~~BLACK &~~ White
im looking in this mirror
and i see you instead of me.

adventure

~~BLACK &~~ White
Wowland

Keasha Gray *August 10, 2010 at 1:29pm*

desire and lust
grows more with each thrust
i cant get enough
insatiable

we're under the sheet
from our head to our feet
every moment is sweet
insatiable

now your on top
im screaming dont stop
my cherry's going to pop
insatiable

i've fallen in love
my heart stolen because
ur a thief without a glove
insatiable

now here i stand
want you as my man
please take my hand
insatiable

~~BLACK~~ & *White*
to be cont...

Keasha Gray *August 11, 2010 at 7:24pm*

i woke up around for with you on my brain even though you were lying next to me i started writing:)

i cant help but think about how much i care.
how much we share.
im not going nowhere.

you know how to fill me with ecstasy.
no need for fantasy.
i love being in your reality.
with you i can be free.
im allowed to be me.

please let your body join with mine.
be my sunshine.
make love one more time.
inspire me to finish this rhyme.....

~~BLACK &~~ White
very good perk

Keasha Gray *August 11, 2010 at 10:44pm*

his point of view:

so i went to orlando
and met some chick.
at first glance i didnt know
she was sick.

but now she needs
a doctor quick.
because this girl
is in love with my dick!

now i did tap that ass
once or twice.
and ill admit
it did feel nice

but she laced my dick
with platnium and ice.
your honor she thinks
she's my dick's wife!

i need a divorce
and i need one fast.
trust me this thing
will not last.

one day she woke up

adventure 11

~~BLACK~~ & White
and maced my face.
then sucked my dick
and baked it a cake!

trust me she's crazy!
I REST MY CASE!

adventure 12

~~BLACK &~~ White
very good perk pt 2

Keasha Gray *August 11, 2010 at 10:46pm*

her point of view:

some chick from orlando?
no dear im your wife.
and we wouldnt be here
if you could get right.

yes i did lace your dick
with platnium and ice.
but not cuz im crazy
i want ALL of you for life.

the mace in your face
was because of a fight.
and how freaking absurd
im your dick's wife!

the cake was for you
because of the fight.
and as i recall
we made love that night.

in love with your dick?
no im in love with you.
but you cant see that
so now we're thru.

you can have your divorce

adventure 13

~~BLACK &~~ White
and yes i'll be hurt.
cause i love you
your dick's just a very good perk;)

adventure 14

~~BLACK &~~ White
thank you

Keasha Gray August 12, 2010 at 11:44am

this was inspired by you but not written for you.
nevertheless you can still have it.

i stand strong in my faith
with my heart in my hand
your grace and your mercies
sent me dexter brockman.

he's warm and caring
he reminds me of you
let no man on earth
come between us two.

may we love unconditionally
just as you do
so the whole world will know
that our love comes from you.

if ever we doubt
that we're going the wrong way
let your love for us
make both of us stay.

may we always take comfort
in each others arms
with confidence that
its you helping us stay strong.

adventure 15

~~BLACK~~ & White
and when the time comes
for our lives here to end
i"ll still praise and thank you
for dexter brockman.

adventure 16

~~BLACK &~~ White
open the door

Keasha Gray August 12, 2010 at 11:46am

fish and grits
on the late night tip
you let me push the whip
when we took the miami trip.

you let me wear your shirt
rough sex but it doesn't hurt
i dont see flaws or little quirks
I'll do anything to make this work.

you gave me so much
and yet i want more
open your hearts door
allow me to explore
maybe take a life long tour.

I'll make sure
unlike others before
that you wont hurt anymore
i wont tamper or toy
nor let it be destroyed.

adventure 17

~~BLACK~~ & *White*
little keasha and her friend

Keasha Gray *August 12, 2010 at 8:06pm*

little keasha had a friend.
keasha's friend was d brockman.

little keasha liked to play
with d brockman every night and day.

they didnt play with kiddie toys
they played a game called girls and boys.

the game is best if played at night
first they get close and cut out the lights.

he gives her a kiss on her lips or her cheek
then unbuttons her shirt cuz her breast taste so sweet.

now its her turn so she grabs hold of his head
then whispers to him "let's get in the bed."

this is where the fun begins
and you can tell who's going to win.

if keasha goes for a ride
and makes d brockman close his eyes.

the game is over, keasha wins
but rest assured they will play again.

if d brockman puts on suffocate or brand new
game over. theres nothing little keasha can do.

adventure 18

~~BLACK~~ & White

*there are only 2 people that play this game
and repeatedly i have said their name.*

*for the record i'll say them once again
it's little keasha and d brockman.*

adventure 19

~~BLACK &~~ White
dexter

Keasha Gray *August 12, 2010 at 10:03pm*
this is far from one of my best but i hope you enjoy it anyway.

dexter, dexter your so cool
i want to kiss you after school.

dexter, dexter sweet and kind
please say that you will always be mine.

dexter, dexter smart and funny
your cuter than the easter bunny.

dexter, dexter your my boo
and i would love to marry you.

in my school girl voice lol

adventure 20

~~BLACK &~~ White
all in my head

Keasha Gray *August 13, 2010 at 12:05am*

desperation has set in. call it my last temptation. i want you tonight. read the poem. call bm #1. tell her there is an extra $20 in her pocket (10 from me and 10 from you) if she keeps them 1 more night.

wowland. speechless. mere words cant explain.
the yearning inside me to scream out your name.

i want "this"...i love "this"....whatever "this" is
daydream "this"...i need "this" feel like dorthy in the whiz.

im trying. im fighting. DAMN this feels nice
the tingles. the jitters. might profess my love tonight.

I LOVE YOU!!! YES I LOVE YOU!!! wait, cant say that to you
hold it in. scratch his back. do whatever you have to do.

it's not just my flesh, my soul screams it too.
it's screaMING! it's screaMING! OH DEX I DO LOVE YOU!!!

i said it. i did it. and i said his name too.
but it was all in your head so he didn't hear you:(

adventure 21

~~BLACK~~ & ~~White~~
the morning after...

Keasha Gray *August 13, 2010 at 10:17am*

there is sunshine there is rain and it all looks the same
last night i said something now somethings have changed.

i told him i love him and screamed out his name
to tell you the truth, i don't feel any shame.

not sure how he feels, its "don't ask don't tell"
cant read his mind, don't know him that well.

maybe one day he will write for me
and explain how he feels in the form of poetry.

i know his situation with the kids and his ex
he keeps me updated via phone calls and text.

i hope and pray his true feelings he will tell
until that day i'll still send his daily in an email.

adventure 22

~~BLACK~~ & White
all you had to do was ask

Keasha Gray August 14, 2010 at 3:18pm

sometimes we must suffer and endure life's pains
but when things get too rough just call out his name.

I know for a fact he will send you relief
and allow you to have some joy and some peace.

there is a verse that was sent just for you
it can be found in Genesis chapter 2.

you've heard it before and you know what it means
scroll down the page and read verse 18.

he knows what you want and he knows what you need
just open your eyes and accept his gift..... PLEASE.

~~BLACK~~ & *White*
patience is a virtue

Keasha Gray *August 17, 2010 at 1:40pm*

I figured it out, you gave me a clue
pretty sure you want me as much as i want you.

seducing my mind and enticing my thoughts
touchdown! your going to give me your heart.

i sent you my love thru poetry
now your showing love right back at me.

in the car you gave me the sticky note
the one with the poem that you wrote.

i sent you a subliminal early one morn'
you responded explaining how you are torn.

i know none of this was part of the plan
but hear me out from a woman to a man:

patience is a virtue.
take as much time as you need to.
to go thru the things your going thru.
but know that my feelings are true.
and in the end i will still want you.

adventure 24

~~BLACK &~~ White
help wanted

Keasha Gray *August 21, 2010 at 11:57am*

The road that I chose may seem a bit rough
with work and kids sometimes things can get tough
I wake up some mornings thinking I've had enough
but my conscience won't let me call my own bluff.

So I struggle and cope but there is never an end
then I struggle and cope all over again
In life it feels like I just can't win
HELP WANTED: IN SEARCH OF A REALLY GOOD FRIEND.

Dear help wanted: in search of a really good friend
i'm someone in which you can depend.
I'm caring and loyal a true friend til the end
and when you need help, a helping hand I'll lend.

my name is Keasha and I'm a single parent too
it seems like i have a lot in common with you
at times I struggle with what I should do
this life feels like a puzzle and I need a clue.

who knows if us meeting was meant to be
who knows if it was destiny
we wont really know unless we try and see
so give me a call at XXX-XXX-3693

adventure 25

~~BLACK &~~ White
repayment

Keasha Gray *August 25, 2010 at 8:31pm*

i cant help but think about you constantly,
and not just thoughts of you on top of me.

our talks, our jokes, our phone conversations,
this is more to me than just sexual relations.

being with you i don't have a care in the world,
you make me feel special like i'm really your girl.

I wish I could repay you for the happiness you give me,
but i'm not rich so please accept my poetry.

may the words I send touch you like seeing a rose starting to bloom,
and place that smile on your face that can light up a crowded room.

and after your day has finally come to an end,
may these same words bring you happiness again.

adventure 26

~~BLACK &~~ White
repentance

Keasha Gray *August 26, 2010 at 5:26pm*

Forgive me father for I have sinned
I told a lie to him again.

two weeks ago i had a dream
and very strange it did seem.

the virgin mother appeared to me
and said i would have two babies.

she flashed a light, one pink then one blue
terrified, I didnt know what to do.

i woke up thinking "how weird was that"
then noticed my stomach was no longer flat.

i wanted to tell him about the dream and the babies
but i know for sure that he'll think i am crazy

i told my priest and he called me blessed
i asked him how with all this stress

at 37 im the mother of 4
and i had somethings done cuz i didnt want anymore.

he said God can forgive almost any sin
and as i recall he gave a child to a virgin.

I called my dr and dex beeped in
so I had to lie to him again.

adventure 27

~~BLACK~~ & White

*my conscience is driving me crazy, this aint fair
i feel this is a cross that i can not bare.*

*please soften his heart to forgive what i've done
and give me my answers at the dr's on 9/1*

adventure 28

~~BLACK~~ & *White*
i wonder

Keasha Gray *August 30, 2010 at 3:20pm*

i wonder what you like to eat.
is it chicken, pork or gator meat?

when you go to church, what do you wear,
and where do you go to cut your hair?

what day of the week is your favorite day,
and when your asleep on which side do you lay?

would you prefer a long walk in the park,
or a booty call when it gets dark?

if you could live anywhere,
where would it be and why would you pick there?

if you had millions what would you do?
buy a house, some clothes and a car or two?

when the road gets rough, i know your tough,
but when do you say enough is enough?

there are so many things that i wonder about you,
and if never answered, i'd still be happy to know but not know you:)

~~BLACK~~ & White
fear of the "L" word

Keasha Gray *September 8, 2010 at 4:57pm*

I miss sharing my thoughts with you
decided to write you a line or two

False Evidence Appearing Real
makes me hide how I really feel.

It's been said that actions speak louder than words
if this is true than every touch makes my feelings heard.

no pressure on you has become my m.o.
i keep telling myself to take things slow.

I know that you have a thousand things on your mind
and sorting them out is going to take time.

a partner right now might drive you insane
the last thing i want is to bring you more pain.

for now i'll just keep my thoughts to myself
because saying i love you might be bad for your health lol.

adventure 30

~~BLACK~~ & ~~White~~
going fishing

Keasha Gray September 9, 2010 at 1:19am

i know you like fishing so i'll use that this time
to explain what i'm trying to say in this rhym.

i was swimming one day and i saw a fishing line
and at first glance it was looking mighty fine.

knowing what happens once i get hooked
i still proceeded to take a closer look.

enticing, intriguing but i cant see the bait
i want to get hooked, but maybe it's too late.

my eyes are now open and i can clearly see
the reason there is no bait is because it wasn't for me.

maybe you didn't feel your line pulling when your bait was took
but from under this water i can see another fish still on your hook.

an experienced fisherman you have to deny
that the fish is still there, that must be a lie.

over the years other fish have tried
but none have succeeded at moving that fish aside.

now your thinking you had this pole and line for so long
that letting go and buying a new one just seems wrong.

adventure 31

~~BLACK &~~ *White*
so what happens next?

your still deceived
the fish doesn't leave.

i get a wish
and make you a fish.

your in the water so the truth you can now see
then you refuse to go back and swim off into the ocean
with me:)
THE END

adventure 32

~~BLACK &~~ *White*

my alter ego

Keasha Gray September 9, 2010 at 12:21pm
i cant take this shit anymore
lights out, clothes off, im locking the door.

after this horrible day i've been thru
my alter ego is coming out and she wants to fuck you.

no kissing no hugging no squeezing and touching
just you and me and a whole lot of fucking.

"get it" get it" in a polite way
naw "fuck me" fuck me" is what i'm going to say.

i'm going to make you cum so quick
and tonight you will know that it's my dick.

i want you to suck it and i dont mean my lips
and i really don't care if you say i'm a trip.

my plans for round two?
i'm going to suck you.
you cum hard in my mouth than scream "damn i love you"

at this point your thirsty and may want a snack.
sorry sexy dex but this chick dont do that
i just like to fuck, that mushy shit is whack
but thanks for the dick now i'll send Keasha back.

adventure 33

~~BLACK~~ & White
me and my boo

Keasha Gray *September 11, 2010 at 10:18am*

tonight is the night i get to see you,
no work, no kids, just me and my boo.

candles and music, it's time for me to unwind
and i hope you don't mind "a little bump and grind"

I have some chocolate syrup and we can use it, I wont bite
or we can take your smart phone and make a movie tonight.

I can spend hours being lost in your smile,
so we could just snuggle and laugh for a while.

or, maybe we'll choose to play it by ear
I really don't care, just as long as your here.

basically, i'm yearning to be with you,
no work, no kids, just me and my boo:)

adventure 34

~~BLACK~~ & *White*
happy birthday 2 me

Keasha Gray October 7, 2010 at 5:57pm
a bubble bath by candle light
to start things off for the night

i love it when a "manly" man
is not afraid to hold my hand

you spread my legs open and i open my eyes
thinking to myself "this is a big surprise"

i have to admit...you got me...i'm sprung
darn that superman with his darn super tongue.

do i have any regrets? i can't say that "i do"
but i can add to my list of reasons i love you.

adventure 35

~~BLACK~~ & *White*
i surrender

Keasha Gray October 7, 2010 at 5:57pm

how can a man armed with two hands and his tongue
no traditonal weapons like a knife or a gun
manage to completely weaken someone
capturing their kingdom, and this battle he has won.

strategecially, i am no match for you
you hit me with things most conquerors don't do
the victory was mine, but know i'm left without a clue
wondering why i have submitted totally unto you.

the licking and sucking, attacking without fear
im suppose to fight back but i want to hold you near
soft music playing in my ear
every lick makes me say "i dont care, i dont care"

so many kisses, you never did this before
my neck, my breast, we are definately at war
how can my enemy be someone i adore
lashing me at will, yet i want more and more.

Damn it! now your licking me in "my spot".
licking it up and down, from the bottom to the top!
keep going. keep going. PLEASE DONT STOP!
make me relinquish every drop.

my toes are curled and the world is standing still
my heart is pounding and my legs i cant feel
i cant believe this feeling is real
sad part is you could do it again at will.

adventure 36

~~BLACK~~ & White

i surrender mighty warrior, i can no longer fight
you have captured my kingdom on this very night.
my weakness exposed, i've lost all of my might
if loving you is wrong, then i dont want to be right.

adventure 37

~~BLACK &~~ White
my bestie

Keasha Gray October 8, 2010 at 12:01pm
i know a guy who is capable of making the grinch laugh
he doesn't hold grudges, he's mastered the art of leaving the past in the past.

he is a good son, brother, cousin and friend
and an awsome father to his four children.
(dee, kera, riya, jayden)

he works a 9-5 but has his own publishing biz
and often lends a helping hand to the mothers of his kids.

i can talk football to him all day and night
and although we cheer for different teams, we never ever fight.

im not going to mention all of the things he has done for me
so let's just say that he knows the meaning of ecstasy.

there are not enough words nor time in a day to explain his greatness to you
but trust and believe that all of the words i put in this poem are true.

if you ever get a chance to meet him, i hope that you will see
why i proclaim to the world that he is my bestie :-)

adventure 38

~~BLACK~~ & ~~White~~
your genie

Keasha Gray October 11, 2010 at 6:02pm
welcome ol' handsome and noble one
i am a genie, are you ready for some fun?

one wish i will grant if you do what i say
and your wish will come true but you MUST obey.

take I-75 to Interstate 4
then follow the gps to your bestie's door. 🚗

go up the stairs and make a right
the room may seem dark but there will be candle light 🕯 .

there will be a lady a little taller than 5'2
laying in the bed, waiting for you. 💆

make love to her while your thinking of your wish
and when you are done, seal your wish with a kiss 💋 .

If you do everything that i instructed you to do
the moment your done, your wish will come true 👍 .

If you don't do everything exactly right,
i'll give you a second chance, come back tomorrow
night 🤍

adventure 39

~~BLACK~~ & White
dear mr. brockman,

Keasha Gray October 12, 2010 at 2:22pm
please try to understand
im still by your side and im still holding your hand

my love and friendship are totally free
there is nothing you have to do for me

tainting me? oh no! thats not true.
confusing is more of a word i would use.

your going thru some things and i wish i could help
but i know you need to solve things yourself.

just drop me a line from time to time
tell me your ok or your not doing too fine.

i don't like to assume or try to guess
communication usually works best.

"somewhere down the line our paths may never meet"
and if it occurs i'll accept that defeat.

your a great man, friend and lover
so happy "our lives will always be impacted by what we have....each other".

love,
your bestie

adventure 40

~~BLACK~~ & *White*
thanks again

Keasha Gray October 27, 2010 at 5:57pm
Sometimes i think your feelings about me are up in the air
then you do something wonderful that shows me you do care

i wasn't expecting those emails but needless to say
they both had me smiling for the rest of the day

was there a subliminal in O-M-G
or was the subliminal in make-a-movie

the lip biting and clarks were a nice touch
its the little things you do that mean so darn much

until the next time i can gaze in your eyes,
much love & thanks for such a wonderful surprise.

adventure 41

~~BLACK~~ & *White*
good morning mr. Brockman

Keasha Gray December 17, 2010

it's been quite some time,
since I've had a chance
to write you a rhyme.

Our schedules have been hectic
no time to play,
but I had to send you a daily
because today is a special day.

We made it to month 5,
and it was not like any of the others.
We remained friends
without sex with one another.

We still talk every night
and text during the day,
Strengthening our bond
without sex getting in the way.

The days, weeks and months
are flying by so fast.
I hope that our future
becomes greater than our past.

Take a moment today
to reminisce on what we've been through
and with any luck,
I'll get some lip-biting from you.

adventure 42

~~BLACK~~ & White

HAPPY 5 MONTHIVERSARY

still loving you

adventure 43

~~BLACK &~~ White
daily

Keasha Gray February 7, 2011 at 6:44pm
Once again Sexy Dex
has inspired me to write.
Good convo stimulates my mind
and there was much stimulation last night.

I'm addicted to the calmness of your voice
some people might call me crazy
The best description I can give
is a mothers voice to her new baby.

Although our homes are far apart
I feel we've grown closer together.
One call from you and a sweet memory of your smile
makes each day feel brighter and better.

We still find ways to talk everyday
and the words flow like an endless sea.
Enjoy your day off, remember my love
and forgive me for not writing you more poetry :-)

adventure 44

www.ingramcontent.com/pod-product-compliance
Lightning Source LLC
Chambersburg PA
CBHW032018290426
44109CB00013B/711